GENETIC CONDITIONS

Alopecia Areata

PETRA MILLER

Cavendish Square

New York

Published in 2016 by Cavendish Square Publishing, LLC
243 5th Avenue, Suite 136, New York, NY 10016

First Edition

Website: cavendishsq.com

CPSIA Compliance Information: Batch #CW16CSQ

All websites were available and accurate when this book was sent to press.

Library of Congress Cataloging-in-Publication Data

Miller, Petra.
Alopecia areata / Petra Miller.
pages cm. — (Genetic conditions)
Includes bibliographical references and index.
ISBN 978-1-5026-0948-9 (hardcover) ISBN 978-1-5026-0949-6 (ebook)
1. Alopecia areata. 2. Baldness. I. Title.
RL155.5.M55 2016
616.5'46—dc23

2015023054

Editorial Director: David McNamara
Editor: Fletcher Doyle
Copy Editor: Nathan Heidelberger
Art Director: Jeffrey Talbot
Designer: Alan Sliwinski
Senior Production Manager: Jennifer Ryder-Talbot
Production Editor: Renni Johnson
Photo Research: J8 Media

Printed in the United States of America

CONTENTS

INTRODUCTION

Alopecia areata is not a deadly disease, so it doesn't get the attention or the funding that other genetic **disorders** do. It is a complex problem and multiple genes are involved, so answers to questions about the disease have been hard to come by. However, recent research has linked alopecia areata to other common genetic diseases, and this could lead to treatments to help people suffering from it.

Alopecia areata is a disease that causes sudden hair loss, usually in round patches. The name, which is Latin, describes the disease. "Alopecia" means "hair loss," or "baldness." "Areata" means "occurring in patches." The disease usually affects the scalp but can affect the rest of the body as well.

Alopecia areata is an **autoimmune** disease. Alopecia areata usually begins as a few small bald patches that appear suddenly on the scalp. The bare skin in the patches looks smooth and normal. Usually, no other **symptoms** accompany the bald patches. Occasionally, however, there is a burning sensation or mild itching, tingling, or tenderness.

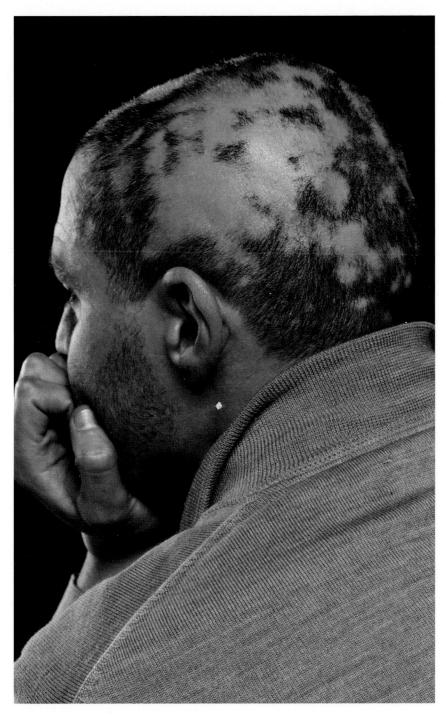

Alopecia areata comes on suddenly, and hair loss usually occurs in circular patches.

The disease's progress varies from person to person, and there is no way to predict what will happen. Some people develop only a few bald patches, regrow their hair within about a year, and never lose hair again. Other people develop many bald patches and lose hair and regrow it over and over again for many years.

There are other forms of alopecia. People with alopecia totalis lose all their scalp hair. People with alopecia universalis lose all the hair on their whole body, including eyebrows, eyelashes, and ear and nose hair. These more severe symptoms strike only 5 percent of people with the disease.

Alopecia areata does not cause physical pain and cannot kill a person. However, it can cause great emotional stress because of its effects on a person's appearance. People with alopecia universalis may suffer more allergies and illnesses because more dust and germs can enter their eyes, nose, and ears.

Alopecia areata can strike anyone. About five million people in the United States have the disease. Most people with the disease experience their first episode of hair loss before the age of twenty. However, about 40 percent suffer their first episode as fully-grown adults.

Regardless of when it sets in, alopecia areata can be an embarrassing disorder that can cause psychological difficulties in people who get it.

Seeking Answers

G ail Porter did not have the looks of a young woman who would have trouble finding romance. She was a model and a presenter on television in Great Britain. Her photos appeared in men's magazines. She dated one rock musician and married another. Then her hair fell out in 2005. Porter had alopecia totalis, a condition in which all of the hair on a person's head falls out.

She lost a lot of her modeling work but continued to present shows on TV despite not wearing a hat or a wig on screen. She also has done charitable work, becoming an ambassador for a group called Little Princess Trust that gives wigs to children who have lost their hair. Divorced the year she lost her hair, she told a British newspaper in November 2014 that at the age of forty-three she feared she would never marry again and suffered from

British television personality Gail Porter lost confidence in her looks when she lost her hair.

insecurity because she was "a funny looking thing." Her hair has come back partially several times but has always fallen out again.

Porter is just one recent, well-known victim of a disease that has a long history. The earliest references to alopecia appear in ancient Greek and Roman writings. Around 400 BCE, the Greek physician Hippocrates (circa 460 BCE–ca. 375 BCE) first used the Greek term *alōpekia*, from which the Latin term alopecia comes. However, he probably was not describing the disease we know today as alopecia areata. "Alōpekia" literally means "fox's disease." Hippocrates may have been referring to **mange**, a disease that is common in foxes. It also occurs in other mammals, including humans. Like alopecia areata, mange causes patchy hair loss. In mange, however, the skin in the bald patches is not smooth and normal. It is red, puffy, and very itchy. Mange is caused by mites, tiny animals that are related to spiders.

More than four centuries after Hippocrates, a Roman writer named Aulus Cornelius Celsus gave the first description of what is clearly the disease we know as alopecia areata. Celsus described two forms of alopecia in a medical encyclopedia titled *De Medicina* that he wrote around 30 CE. One form was complete baldness that occurred in people of all ages. The second was a winding pattern of bald patches across the scalp. Celsus called this form *ophiasis,* which means "snake," because the winding pattern reminded him of a snake. He incorrectly wrote that ophiasis occurred only in children.

The name "alopecia areata" was not used until many centuries after Hippocrates and Celsus. The first person to use it was a French physician named François Boissier de Sauvages de la Croix. It appeared in a book he published in 1763 titled *Nosologia Methodica.* This book was an early attempt to classify diseases, or organize them into groups.

Breakthrough

Dr. Henry Kunkel and his coworkers prove that people with rheumatoid arthritis have antibodies in their blood that act against other antibodies as if they were antigens (toxins or foreign substances). This causes inflammation in the joints of these patients. This 1950s discovery proves the existence of autoimmune diseases.

Hair loss in foxes is a symptom of mange, which is caused by mites. Mange has no connection to alopecia areata.

Many others like it followed. Since little was known about the causes of diseases, these books grouped diseases according to their symptoms.

TWO IDEAS ON THE CAUSE

As medical knowledge grew, physicians attempted to identify the cause of alopecia areata. By the late 1800s, two main **hypotheses** had emerged. One was that an infection caused by **parasites** produced the disease. The other was that a nerve-related disorder caused it.

Physicians who believed the parasite hypothesis pointed out that the area of hair loss slowly expanded in size. This is exactly what would happen if there were an infection at the site of hair loss. Physicians also noticed that institutions like schools and orphanages often seemed to have large numbers of cases of alopecia areata. This was what would be expected if there were an infection that was spreading from person to person. Discoveries that parasites caused other diseases, such as ringworm, made the parasite hypothesis for alopecia areata seem like a good explanation. Nevertheless, physicians were unable to identify a specific parasite that might cause alopecia areata.

Other physicians supported the idea that a nerve-related disorder caused alopecia areata. This hypothesis was known as the trophoneurotic, neurotrophic, or **neuropathic** hypothesis. All these names refer to nerves that do not function properly. The cause of the problem was thought to be emotional stress

The accumulation of unpaid bills is one of the many stress producers that can trigger alopecia areata.

or physical damage to the nerves, which harmed **hair follicles**. Most dermatologists, or skin doctors, came to believe that a nervous disorder was probably the cause of alopecia areata. In support of this hypothesis, they pointed to the fact that people who had recently developed alopecia areata frequently displayed emotional stress. However, it often was unclear if stress was caused by the hair loss or the other way around.

New Kind of Disease

The role of stress in causing alopecia areata is now understood more clearly. However, understanding the physical factors behind the condition took decades to discover.

Back in 1891, a study published in a French journal had shown that cells from the immune system invaded hair follicles affected by alopecia areata. This was the first hint that alopecia areata might be an autoimmune disease. However, no one at the time could have recognized that. In 1891, the concept of autoimmune disease did not exist. It was not until the 1950s and 1960s that most physicians came to accept the idea of autoimmune diseases. In 1957, Dr. Ernest Witebsky of the University at Buffalo's School of Medicine co-authored a paper in which he set out criteria for autoimmune diseases. These were called Witebsky's postulates.

Autoimmunity is an immune response directed toward a toxin or other foreign substance in the body that scientists call an antigen. The response is usually the production of antibodies to battle the antigen. An autoimmune disease is one caused completely or in part by the immune system making a mistake and attacking healthy substances that belong in the body.

Common Disorders

The National Institutes of Health (NIH) estimates that 5 to 8 percent of people living in the United States have an autoimmune disorder. These disorders usually last for the lifetime of the person and need constant or regular care. Some of the most common autoimmune diseases don't show up until later in a person's life. Here are some of the most common autoimmune diseases and their symptoms:

Graves Disease: The thyroid gland becomes too active, so people have trouble sleeping, lose weight, become irritable, and develop eyes that bulge, a sensitivity to heat, weakness in their muscles, and shakiness in their hands.

Lupus: An attack by antibodies on the body causes rashes, sensitivity to the sun, swelling and damaged joints and organs, and joint pain.

Type I Diabetes: An attack on the cells in the pancreas that produce insulin leaves patients unable to process glucose, so they get high blood sugar. This is called hyperglycemia. This leads to an increased risk of kidney failure, loss of eyesight, heart disease, circulation problems, and stroke.

Multiple Sclerosis: An attack on the central nervous system can cause balance problems, muscle weakness, trouble speaking, difficulty with walking, tremors, and paralysis.

Rheumatoid Arthritis: An attack on tissues in the joints leads to muscle pain, fatigue, deformed joints, weakness, and the loss of appetite and weight.

Joanna Rowsell (*right*), who won a silver medal with her Great Britain teammates at the Track Cycling World Championships in February 2015, began losing her hair at age ten.

It is estimated by the National Institutes of Health (NIH) that there are at least eighty human diseases in which autoimmune responses play a primary or secondary role.

It was only in the 1980s that many physicians and scientists began to think that alopecia areata might be an autoimmune disease. Today, it is medically accepted that a person's immune system mistakes hair follicles for dangerous invaders and attacks them with white blood cells, causing hair loss. Three pieces of evidence support this hypothesis. First, some people with

Alopecia Areata

alopecia areata regrow hair when they are given drugs that are meant to affect the immune system. This suggests that the immune system is somehow involved in alopecia areata. Second, some people with alopecia areata have more antibodies in their blood than normal. Antibodies are substances that are produced by the immune system when it is trying to defend the body against invaders. Third, cells from the immune system that are not usually found in hair follicles are found in the follicles of people with alopecia areata.

It has also been discovered that people with alopecia areata are more likely than other people to have another autoimmune disease or to have a family member with an autoimmune disease. About 20 percent of people with alopecia areata have a family member with the disorder. This raises two questions: Why do some people get alopecia and others do not? Why do autoimmune diseases often run in families? The answers lie partly in genetics.

Complex Problem

Some genetic disorders are caused by a single gene and are called single gene disorders. Among these disorders are cystic fibrosis, Huntington's disease, and muscular dystrophy. These types of disorders are rare.

Most genetic problems are complex disorders, such as heart disease and diabetes. They are caused by a combination of multiple genetic and environmental problems. They are **polygenic**. A person must have the right combination of genetic factors to inherit the disease. Because there are many factors that go into passing on complex disorders, they are called multifactorial.

What is not complex is this fact: genes are the basic units of **heredity**. Every living cell contains genes. They are found on structures called **chromosomes**, which are made of proteins and

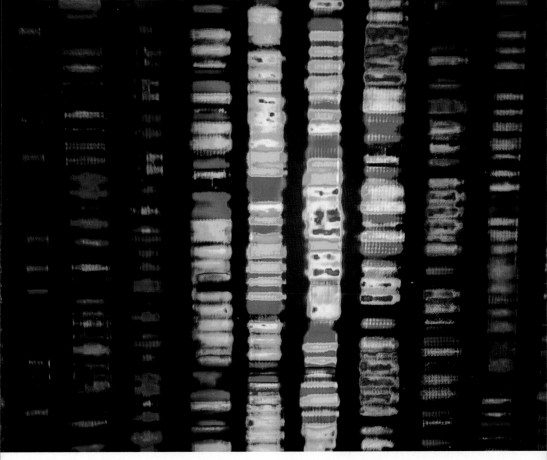

The DNA sequence is the ordering of the four bases that make up a molecule of DNA. The order creates a code that directs the body's production of proteins. By reading a sequence, scientists can tell how proteins are made.

deoxyribonucleic acid, or DNA. An organism's complete set of DNA is known as its **genome**. Individual genes are stretches of the genome's DNA that tell the cell how to make the proteins necessary for life. Genes make up only part of the genome. The rest of the DNA in the genome performs functions not involved with heredity.

Different living things have different numbers of genes and chromosomes. It is thought that humans have approximately twenty-five thousand genes, which are arranged on twenty-three pairs of chromosomes. Each person inherits one set of

Complex Problem

twenty-three chromosomes from his or her mother and one set from his or her father. The genes on these chromosomes determine such things as what color hair and eyes the person will have and how tall the person will be. They also determine whether the person will have a genetic disease (or be **susceptible** to developing one). Physicians and scientists know all these things now, but for most of human history, heredity was a great mystery. Most of what is known about genetics has been learned in the last century or so.

EARLY GENETIC RESEARCH

The story actually starts in the second half of the 1800s, when improved microscopes led to the discovery of chromosomes in cells. Before then, scientists did not know such structures existed. By the late 1800s, studies of cells and cell reproduction had led some scientists to believe that chromosomes were the basis of heredity. However, that idea was not widely accepted. Then, in 1909, Thomas Hunt Morgan and a team of scientists began studying genetics using fruit flies. The men wanted to study the inheritance of traits over several generations, and fruit flies were the perfect subjects to study. They mature and reproduce quickly, giving scientists several generations to

 Breakthrough

Scientist S. Giovannini finds leukocytes (white blood cells that help fight disease) in hair follicles of people with alopecia in 1891. These leukocytes destroy the hair bulb, causing the hair to fall out.

Alopecia Fact Sheet

Alopecia areata is an autoimmune skin disease resulting in the loss of hair on the scalp and elsewhere on the body. Here are a few facts about the disorder:

» It is estimated that Alopecia areata will affect about two percent of the population, or about 5 million people in the United States alone and 145 million people worldwide.

» Alopecia areata occurs in males and females of all ages and races.

» Some persons are more genetically susceptible to developing alopecia areata, which involves multiple genes.

» In at least one out of five persons with alopecia areata, someone else in their family also has it.

» Eight genes related to alopecia areata have been discovered that are related to Type 1 diabetes, rheumatoid arthritis, and celiac disease.

» There appear to be two forms of alopecia areata—an early-onset form and a late-onset form. Those who develop their alopecia areata in childhood typically have alopecia totalis or alopecia universalis later in life; this early-onset form is usually more chronic.

Source: National Alopicia Areata Foundation.

study in just a short time. Morgan and his team studied the inheritance of traits such as eye color and wing shape. Their work provided the first proof that genes are the units of heredity. It also showed that genes are located on chromosomes.

Mutations, or genetic changes, often appeared in Morgan's fruit flies. By studying these mutations, Morgan and his team were able to determine what traits each gene affected. They were also able to determine where each gene was located. In other words, they made the first genetic map.

Even with the discoveries made by Morgan and his team, little was known about the function and structure of genes and chromosomes. Important advances were made in the 1940s. Early in that decade, George W. Beadle and Edward L. Tatum carried out genetic experiments with a fungus. They discovered that genes control chemical reactions in cells by directing the production of special proteins called enzymes. The two men also determined that there is one specific gene for each enzyme. Beadle and Tatum's work provided important information about how genes work. However, it still was not clear which part of the material found in chromosomes made up the genes.

KEY TO HEREDITY

Scientists had known for a long time that chromosomes were made up of DNA and proteins. In 1869, Johann Friedrich Miescher discovered DNA, which he called nuclein, during his studies of white blood cells. At the time, no one thought this discovery was very important. Proteins are essential to life processes, and most scientists believed that the proteins in chromosomes were the basis of heredity. Then, in 1944, a team

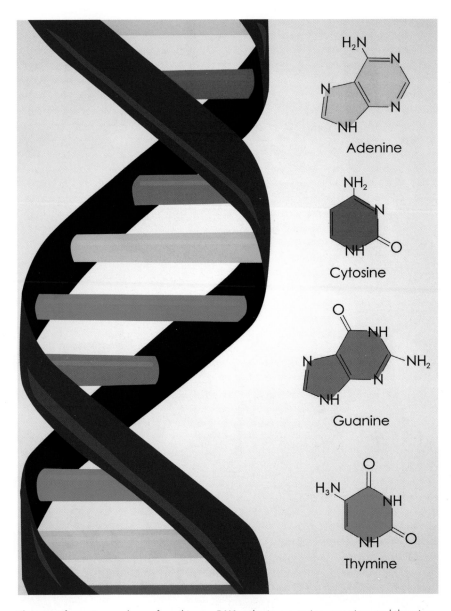

There are four nitrogen bases found in our DNA: adenine, cytosine, guanine, and thymine. Adenine bonds only to thymine, and cytosine bonds only with guanine. When these bases pair, they form the rungs of the ladder in our DNA.

Complex Problem

Dr. James D. Watson helped discover the double helix shape of DNA in the 1950s.

Alopecia Areata

of scientists led by Oswald T. Avery carried out experiments on DNA from bacteria. Their work showed that DNA alone determines heredity. Following this discovery, scientists began to focus research on learning more about DNA.

DNA consists of chemical building blocks called nucleotides. Each nucleotide has three parts: a compound called a phosphate, a sugar called deoxyribose, and a nitrogenous compound called a base. All nucleotides have the same phosphate and sugar. There are four different bases: adenine (A), guanine (G), thymine (T), and cytosine (C). Nucleotides can be arranged in any order on the DNA molecule. The sequence of nucleotides in the DNA determines the genetic code.

In 1953, James Watson and Francis Crick proposed that the structure of DNA was a double helix, a shape resembling a ladder twisted into a spiral. Watson and Crick's model shows how DNA is copied. Each kind of nucleotide bonds with only one other kind of nucleotide. The adenine-containing nucleotide pairs with only the thymine-containing nucleotide, and the guanine-containing nucleotide fits with only the cytosine-containing nucleotide. So, A pairs only with T, and vice versa; C pairs only with G, and vice versa. Research has shown that this model is correct.

The nucleotides in DNA are arranged in groups of three, called **codons**. Each codon instructs the cell to make an **amino acid**. A series of amino acids makes up a protein. After the work of Watson and Crick, the next big challenge in genetics research was learning to read this code, or determining which codon corresponds to each amino acid.

In 1961, Marshall W. Nirenberg discovered the genetic code for one amino acid. In following years, Nirenberg and other scientists determined the codes for all twenty amino acids used to build proteins in humans. Being able to read a gene's code meant scientists could begin to understand the gene's function. It also meant they could recognize when there was a mutation in the gene.

CRACKING THE GENETIC CODE

Researchers developed new methods for studying genes in the 1970s. They discovered how to remove genes from one organism and insert them into another organism. Because this technique recombines DNA from one organism with DNA from another, it is known as recombinant DNA technology. Experiments with recombinant DNA technology have helped scientists learn more about both the structure and function of genes.

As a result of the research done over the course of the twentieth century, physicians and scientists knew quite a bit about genes by the 1980s. This knowledge provided a starting point for researchers who wanted to study genetic diseases. Much of this knowledge, however, came from research carried out on organisms other than humans. Therefore, the information scientists gathered about genes and heredity had to do with general principles that apply to the genes of all living things. Much was still unknown about the specific genes that humans have. Gaining that knowledge became the next big goal in genetic research.

In 1990, the NIH and the **US Department of Energy** (DOE) jointly launched the Human Genome Project. Aided by international organizations, the NIH and DOE began the task of determining the sequence of the nucleotides in human

DNA and identifying all the genes in the human genome. This was an enormous undertaking. In spite of the challenges, researchers working on the project were able to meet their goals ahead of schedule. By 2003, they had established the sequence of nucleotides in the entire human genome.

The Human Genome Project provided a tool for identifying new genes and their function. It is called genetic mapping. To create a genetic map, scientists isolate the DNA from tissue or blood samples of family members who share a disease or trait. They examine this DNA for unique patterns. These patterns are called markers, and they can tell researchers the approximate location of a gene on the chromosome. Using these markers, researchers can map the locations of the genes.

Mapping has helped researchers find the location of genes involved in single gene inherited disorders such as cystic fibrosis. It is helping scientists locate the many genes that play a role in the more common disorders, such as alopecia areata, asthma, and heart disease.

Stressed
Out

A t first glance, forward Charlie Villanueva looks like many other players in the National Basketball Association (NBA). He is tall and muscular, and his head is bald, which puts him in the company of great players such as Michael Jordan.

But when you look closely, you realize it is not only Villanueva's scalp that is missing hair. He is not like Mike. Villanueva does not have eyebrows, either. In fact, he doesn't have hair anywhere. Villanueva has alopecia universalis. He experienced his first episode of hair loss when he was ten years old. He had recurring episodes of hair loss and regrowth until he was thirteen, when his hair fell out and never grew back.

The disease has not stopped Villanueva from achieving success. He was a star basketball player at the University of Connecticut, playing on a National Collegiate Athletic

Basketball player Charlie Villanueva lifts the spirits of children with alopecia areata during meet and greets that are held around the country.

Association championship team in 2004. He was picked in the first round, seventh overall, of the 2005 NBA draft by the Toronto Raptors. He made the playoffs for the first time in his tenth season while playing for the Dallas Mavericks.

What he has done off the court has been more important than any points he scored while on it. Villanueva has served as the spokesperson for the Charlie's Angels Alopecia Areata Awareness Project, which is sponsored by the National Alopecia Areata Foundation (NAAF). As the spokesperson, he takes part in meet and greets with NAAF members in cities around the country. At these events he meets with children and adults, signs autographs, poses for photos, and has conversations with people struggling with the condition.

HARD TO COPE

Alopecia areata is a difficult disease to deal with emotionally. Hair loss for any reason is hard on all people. Men associate baldness with aging and a loss of physical attractiveness. However, studies show that women are more vulnerable to the psychological effects of hair loss than men. Often with women, their hair is part of their identity. When they lose their hair, they can lose self-esteem.

Androgenic alopecia, which is also known as male pattern baldness, is the most common cause of baldness. In men, it shows in a receding hairline and a thinning of hair on the crown. In women, it can show as thinning hair without a receding hairline. This kind of alopecia is genetic and is multifactorial. Men have this condition much more often than women do. The reason is that enzymes convert testosterone, the main male sex **hormone**, into dihydrotestosterone. This hormone makes hair shorter and thinner, and the amount each person has is hereditary.

Women have less testosterone, so they don't lose hair in the same way. Androgenic alopecia in women is related to the action of hormones. Among the factors that can alter these actions are ovarian cysts, use of high androgen index birth control pills, pregnancy, and menopause. At menopause, the amount of estrogen in a woman drops so testosterone can have a greater effect on women at that time. This is why women experience hair loss later in life than men.

Women who suffer emotionally from hair loss often use wigs to restore their self-image.

The loss of hair due to androgenic alopecia is usually gradual. With alopecia areata, it can be rapid. Hair falls out in patches, usually in clumps the size of a quarter. No one knows when or if the hair loss will stop.

Common Problems

The group Bald Girls Do Lunch is a support group for women dealing with alopecia areata. According to its website, blog.baldgirlsdolunch.org, it offers woman a social environment "where they'll never feel strange, different, or alone."

The group lists these problems as common among women with alopecia areata:

» They have a feeling of vulnerability and a fear of rejection by others, from strangers to their husbands.

» They have an altered self-image and a loss of confidence.

» They isolate themselves from others rather than constantly explaining their condition, and this brings on feelings of loneliness, lack of support, and depression.

» They suffer from financial difficulties because health insurance plans don't cover wigs and other ways of hiding hair loss. Out of pocket expenses can create financial stress and guilt because of the high cost of the condition.

» They feel hopeless because there isn't an effective cure for the condition.

» They feel self-conscious because they attract attention when all they want to do is fit in.

Researchers have not yet identified the triggers for alopecia areata, but several possible triggers have been proposed. One of these is stress, which should sound familiar because it was among the possible causes of alopecia areata proposed in the 1800s. However, the theory in the 1800s was that stress directly caused alopecia areata. The modern theory, on the other hand, is that stress triggers an immune response that leads to the autoimmune disease.

There are many psychological problems associated with alopecia areata. It can cause anxiety, depression, social phobias, and intense emotional suffering, and it can lead to personal, social, and work-related problems. The National Institutes of Health stated on its website that "there is an important link between hair and identity, especially for women. About 40 percent of women with alopecia have had marital problems as a consequence, and about 63 percent claim to have had career-related problems."

Other possible triggers include physical injury, infection caused by a virus or bacteria, allergies, or other stressful life events such as the loss of a job. These are all things that can prompt a response from the immune system in both men and women. Using the latter as an example, women who experience times of high stress are found to be eleven times more likely to lose hair than women in the general population. This points out a pattern that people with alopecia areata have difficulty breaking. Stress can trigger alopecia. And alopecia can cause stress that keeps people from recovering from the condition.

Former Mrs. Washington International Cari Bickley, who lost all of her hair to alopecia, receives a lot of support from her husband, Rick.

UNPREDICTABLE PROGRESS

Symptoms of the disease vary greatly. Some people have only one or a small number of bald patches on the scalp or elsewhere on the body. Others may have numerous bald patches. Still others may suffer alopecia totalis, the complete loss of scalp hair. In alopecia universalis, the most severe form of the disease, people lose all hair from their scalp, face, and body. Fingernails and toenails may also be affected, developing dents or grooves, or becoming misshapen. Sometimes nails even fall out.

The course of alopecia areata is unpredictable. Some people experience an episode of patchy hair loss followed by regrowth and never experience hair loss again. Others experience recurring episodes of hair loss and regrowth over many years. For a small number of people, the disease progresses to alopecia totalis or alopecia universalis.

People who have patchy hair loss on just a small area of the scalp usually experience regrowth in about a year, with or without treatment. Those with widespread hair loss are more likely to experience recurring episodes. People who have extensive hair loss and experienced their first episode before they were five years old are less likely to have **spontaneous** regrowth or to respond well to treatment. The same is true of people whose nails are affected or who have **atopy**. If patchy hair loss is going to progress to alopecia totalis, it usually does so within about four months of the first hair loss. Researchers believe that people who have alopecia totalis or alopecia universalis for longer than two years are much less likely to experience spontaneous regrowth

 Breakthrough

Researchers identify a mouse model for alopecia areata in 1991. Dr. John Sundberg, the lead researcher on the project, is able to reproduce the disease in the mice in order to study the disease and search for treatments. A nearly identical mouse model for human adult onset alopecia areata is identified in 2004.

of hair. They are also less likely to respond well to treatment. However, even in cases of alopecia universalis that have lasted several years, spontaneous regrowth can occur.

About 60 percent of people with alopecia areata experience their first episode of hair loss before they are twenty years old.

There have even been reports of babies born with alopecia areata. In the United States alone, nearly five million people have experienced episodes of hair loss caused by alopecia areata.

Many people find that it is very helpful to share their thoughts and feelings with others who have the disease, with people like Charlie Villanueva. Support groups offer one of the best ways to do this. They provide a sense of understanding and acceptance that people with alopecia areata may not find in other places. Support groups also offer an opportunity to get practical advice from people who have gone through the same thing. In addition, they may be a valuable source of information for people who need professional counseling to develop self-confidence and a positive self-image.

The National Alopecia Areata Foundation (NAAF) has support groups around the world and can help people find the nearest group. The foundation's website also offers a special interactive section for young people. There, teens can give and receive advice about dealing with alopecia areata and communicate with other teens from around the world.

Steps
Forward

One of the most important advancements in alopecia areata research was the discovery by Dr. John P. Sundberg of a mouse model for the disease in 1991. Medical researchers use mice because their behavioral, biological, and genetic characteristics are very similar to those of a human. Mice breed rapidly, so many are available for research, and colonies are inbred, reducing genetic variations that might change the outcome of diseases.

Also, many medical conditions experienced by humans can be replicated in mice. Dr. Sundberg uses the mice with alopecia areata in his research at the Jackson Laboratory in Bar Harbor, Maine. These mice have allowed researchers to observe how alopecia areata starts and how it progresses.

Researchers have learned a lot about the progress of alopecia areata by studying mouse models.

Research into the causes and treatment of alopecia areata had dramatically increased before Dr. Sundberg made his discovery. In 1985, the National Alopecia Areata Foundation (NAAF) in San Rafael, California, awarded its first two research grants, each for $5,000. The foundation, which was established in 1981, is an internationally known center for alopecia areata. It funds research, provides information to patients and their families, and organizes workshops and conferences for alopecia areata researchers and for people with the disease. Today, the NAAF is one of two major sources of funding in the United States for alopecia areata research. The other is the National Institutes of Health, a federal government agency that is devoted to medical research.

In the early years, research into alopecia areata was limited by the lack of an animal model. This changed with Sundberg's discovery in 1991.

CREATING A DATABASE

Another important step for current and future research was taken in 2001. That year, the NIH established the National Alopecia Areata Registry. The registry is a database of information taken from thousands of people with alopecia areata and their families. In addition to written records, the registry includes blood samples—which can be used for genetic research—and digital photographs of the scalps of people with alopecia areata. All this information is available to researchers studying the genetics of alopecia areata as well as other aspects of the disease. Information gathered from such a large and varied group of people allows researchers to carry out the kind of genetic analysis that would not be possible otherwise. The registry is located at the University of Texas MD Anderson Cancer Center in Houston, Texas. Other centers involved in collecting data are the University of Colorado; the University of California, San Francisco; the University of Minnesota; and Columbia University in New York City.

Dr. Vera H. Price, a well-known alopecia areata expert, is the cofounder of the National Alopecia Areata Foundation. She served on the foundation's board of directors from its founding in 1981 until 2003. She also serves on the NAAF's Scientific Advisory Council. Dr. Price is a physician, professor

Dr. Vera Price, a leader in alopecia areata research, has been testing ways to form new hair follicles.

of dermatology, and researcher. In her research, she has studied how genes and the immune system relate to alopecia areata. She has also studied how hormones affect hair follicles in common balding. She has been working with **stem cells** in the hair follicle and with forming new hair follicles. This is significant because scientists once believed that we are born with all the hair follicles we will ever have.

The biggest piece of the alopecia areata puzzle came when the Human Genome Project was completed. Without this information, scientists were unable to fully understand complex diseases such as alopecia areata in which multiple genes are involved.

Breakthrough

Eight genes associated with alopecia areata are discovered in 2009. Dr. Angela Christiano identifies a gene (ULBP3) in hair follicles of people with alopecia areata that is not present in the follicles of unaffected people. The protein from ULBP3 starts a chain reaction that leads to hair loss.

Dr. Angela Christiano studies hair at the Columbia University Medical Center. She had been studying hair loss diseases in which only one gene was a factor. Eight such genes have been found. After the genome project was completed, she was able to compare the DNA of one thousand patients from the alopecia registry against a control group of one thousand people who did not have the disease.

Using that information, Christiano and her researchers found 139 markers for the disease. In 2009, she announced she had found the genes responsible for alopecia areata.

COMMON TREATMENTS

Several treatments are currently available, though they do not work equally well for everyone. These treatments are intended to promote new hair growth. They will not cure alopecia areata

Canadian Madeline Urbina, a nineteen-year-old from Ontario with alopecia, had her head decorated with elaborate henna designs in March 2015. Henna is a special dye used to paint images on skin.

and will not prevent new bald patches from developing. The treatments are most effective in mild cases of the disease.

Powerful **anti-inflammatory** drugs called corticosteroids are often used to treat alopecia areata. These drugs work by suppressing the immune system. They are chemically similar to a hormone called cortisol that is produced in the body. Corticosteroids are taken by mouth to treat many autoimmune diseases. However, when taken this way, they can cause serious side effects, such as high blood pressure. As a result, they are not often taken by mouth to treat alopecia areata. Instead, a dermatologist uses a tiny needle to inject corticosteroids into the skin in and around the bald patches. The injections are given once a month, and if they work, new hair growth is visible in one or two months. This method is effective for most people. However, the injections can be painful, so this treatment is not recommended for children.

Topical minoxidil is safe and easy to use. Although scientists do not really understand how minoxidil works, a 5 percent topical minoxidil solution applied twice a day promotes hair regrowth. It is effective in both children and adults and can be applied to the scalp, eyebrows, and beard area. New hair growth usually appears in about twelve weeks.

Another topical treatment for alopecia areata involves anthralin cream or ointment. Anthralin, a synthetic, tarlike substance, is applied to the bald patches once a day and washed off after thirty to sixty minutes. Scientists are not sure exactly how anthralin works, but they believe it suppresses the immune system. For some people with alopecia areata, it can cause new hair growth in eight to twelve weeks.

Scientists will also be trying to find better ways to administer topical treatments for alopecia areata. Using current methods, not all of the medicine applied to the skin of the affected area reaches the hair follicles. Scientists hope to find a substance that will penetrate the fat under the skin to deliver the medicine directly to the hair follicles. Research has already shown that tiny synthetic spheres called **liposomes** do this in research animals. When tested on humans, liposomes in skin creams did not work.

One drug that was found to be effective in reversing general hair loss comes with a warning. Finasteride, which comes in pill form, blocks the conversion of testosterone into dihydrotestosterone, which thins hair and contributes to hair loss. However, this can harm sexual functioning in males and the side effects can last long after the drug is stopped. Pregnant women are warned against using the drug because male **embryos** need dihydrotestosterone to develop their sexual organs.

ALTERNATIVE METHODS

Topical **immunotherapy** is often used to treat adult patients with extensive hair loss. This type of treatment involves applying chemicals that cause a response from the immune system—an allergic reaction usually resulting in an itchy rash. Two chemicals commonly used for this are known as diphencyprone (DPCP) and squaric acid dibutyl ester (SADBE). Scientists think these drugs, which are not approved by the US Food and Drug Administration (FDA), get the immune system to attack the rash rather than hair follicles. About 40 percent of patients treated with topical immunotherapy experience new hair growth in three to twelve months.

Photochemotherapy, sometimes called PUVA, is another treatment used for adult patients with extensive hair loss. The patient is given a drug called psoralen, which causes skin to be very sensitive to **ultraviolet** (UV) rays. These are the rays that make the sun's light damaging to skin. One or two hours later, the patient is exposed to an ultraviolet light source such as a tanning booth. The effectiveness of PUVA treatments is still debated and there are side effects, such as skin cancer. Moreover, people who stop the treatments usually experience hair loss again.

Advances in medical research may make some of these treatments obsolete.

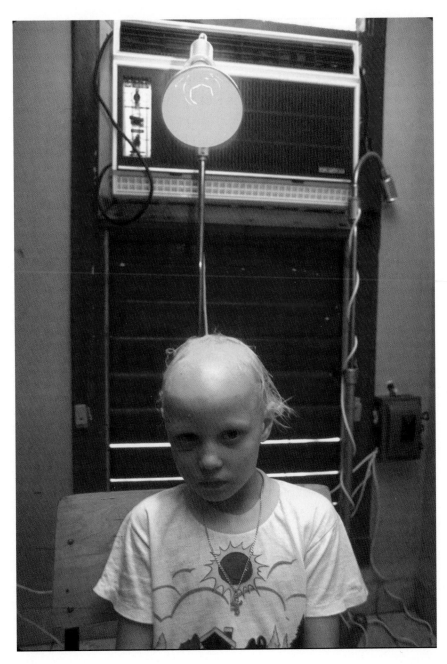

Ultraviolet light is sometimes used to fight hair loss in people with alopecia.

Advancements in Alopecia Areata

30 CE   Roman writer Aulus Cornelius Celsus writes the first description of what is clearly the disease we know as alopecia areata.

1763   French physician François Boissier de Sauvages de la Croix is the first person to use the term "alopecia areata."

1891   A study published in a French journal shows that hair follicles affected by alopecia areata have been invaded by cells from the immune system.

1909   Working with fruit flies, Thomas Hunt Morgan discovers that genes are the units of heredity. His studies lead to the first genetic map.

1950s   Physicians accept the idea that there are autoimmune diseases.

1970s   Recombinant DNA technology is developed. Scientists begin to explore the idea that genes play a role in autoimmune diseases.

1980s   Scientists begin to think that alopecia areata may be an autoimmune disease. Researchers begin to look for the genes that may be involved in alopecia areata.

- 1981   The National Alopecia Areata Foundation is founded.

- 1997   Dr. Angela Christiano identifies the human hairless gene, which is believed to be responsible for a rare genetic alopecia-type disease.

- 2001   The National Alopecia Areata Registry is established.

- 2003   Scientists involved in the Human Genome Project complete their work in determining the sequence of all the nucleotides in the human genome.

- 2004   John P. Sundberg discovers a nearly identical mouse model for adult onset alopecia areata that is useful for examining treatments. Sundberg had found the first mouse model of alopecia areata in 1991.

- 2009   Dr. Christiano discovers the genes implicated in alopecia areata; the T cells that attack hair follicles are identified.

- 2014   The drug ruxolitinib is found to restore the hair of patients in four to five months; researchers find that antigen-specific immunotherapy can convert T cells from being aggressive toward healthy tissue to being protective of that tissue.

Enlightening Connections

D r. Angela Christiano is one of the leading researchers in the genetics of alopecia areata. She also has the condition. Dr. Christiano learned she had alopecia areata at the beauty parlor. She had just arrived at the Columbia University Medical Center, was starting a lab there, and was going through a divorce. All of these conditions cause stress. She said in an interview with the *New York Times* that her hairdresser told her she had a big patch of hair missing on the back of her head. This observation was confirmed by a coworker at the lab.

She was told at a clinic that she had alopecia areata and that there was not much they could do to treat it. Dr. Christiano went through a difficult period and tried to cover her hair loss with careful combing. Her hair loss stopped after two years, and she began her research into developing treatments for the disease.

Dr. Angela Christiano suffered through hair loss due to alopecia areata. Among her contributions is locating the genes that cause the condition.

Her discovery of areas on two chromosomes that are linked to alopecia areata generated great excitement. This marked the first significant evidence of genetic susceptibility for alopecia areata that had been identified as the result of a whole genome analysis.

Locating a Problem

One gene Christiano found, known as ULBP3, is normally not present in hair follicles. However, high concentrations of ULBP3 proteins were found in follicles affected by alopecia areata.

For the immune system to function properly, it has to be able to distinguish between normal parts of a person's body and invaders that could be dangerous. T cells are an important part of the immune system. There are two types of T cells. Helper T cells direct immune responses. Killer T cells, which are also called cytotoxic T cells, hunt down and destroy damaged cells when they are activated by helper T cells. They fight infection.

The immune system recognizes structures called antigens. Every organism, including humans, has its own distinct antigens. The cytotoxic T cells send out T-cell receptors that recognize antigens attached to a cell and they kill the damaged cell. The immune system does not attack things in a person's body that have antigens that identify them as "self." It attacks only things it recognizes as foreign. There are also some parts of the body that are protected from attack because the immune system simply doesn't "see" them. The immune system cannot read the antigens on these parts of the body, so it ignores them. Scientists describe these areas as having an immune privilege.

Breakthrough

A link is found in 2013 between variations in specific genes and the amount of antibodies a person produces. The amount of antibodies in your adaptive immune system influences your ability to fight disease, but having too many antibodies in your system increases your chances of getting an autoimmune disease. This information could lead to individual treatments for overactive immune system responses.

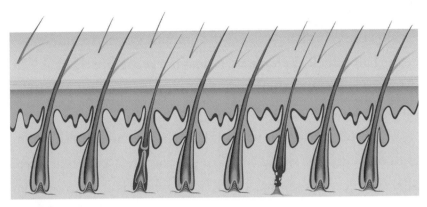

Healthy

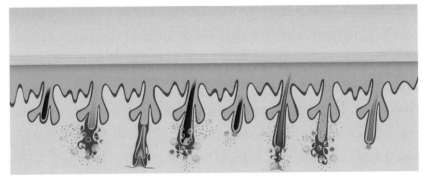

Alopecia areata

Healthy hair follicles, protected by immune privilege, keep their size and ability to grow hair. Immune privilege is removed by a protein in alopecia patients, and the body's immune system attacks the healthy follicles as if they are foreign bodies, destroying them.

There are good reasons for some parts of the body to have immune privilege. It protects organs in the body from some of the reactions to infection, such as swelling, that could damage the organ. One example is the eye, which has immune privilege. If the front chamber of the eye were to swell, that could lead to blindness. Hair follicles have this special protection, too. It is easy to see why this protection is needed in mammals. Although humans do not need their hair to survive, loss of hair would be fatal to polar bears, reindeer, or seals.

However, if a change causes the immune system to suddenly see the hair follicles in humans, it does not recognize them as "self" because it has never seen their antigens before. Immune privilege is lost. So the immune system attacks the antigens it hasn't seen.

This is what happens when ULBP3 is present in follicles. It sends out a distress signal, attracting cytotoxic T cells that have a killer cell receptor, known as NKG2D, which is also involved in other autoimmune disorders. These T cells attack healthy tissue, even though no infection or damage is present.

Dr. Christiano's analysis led her to another discovery. It had been thought that alopecia was somehow related to psoriasis and vitiligo, which are other autoimmune skin diseases. However, psoriasis and vitiligo share almost no genes with alopecia areata. Instead, alopecia areata shares genetic links with celiac disease, type 1 diabetes, and rheumatoid arthritis.

The discovery of the link between alopecia areata and these other autoimmune diseases gives researchers a chance at starting clinical drug trials for alopecia areata earlier than expected. Organs that express NKG2D to start the immune response seem to share a mechanism. There are drugs being tested to treat celiac disease, diabetes and rheumatoid arthritis as well as other diseases where the NKG2D receptor is involved. Researchers have been testing some of these to treat alopecia.

Hair Restored

In 2004, after a five-year study, a second mouse match was identified. This mouse was a virtual identical model for human adult onset alopecia areata. Using these mice, researchers traced the distress signal backwards and were able to find the T cells that were attacking hair follicles. Then, using both mice and human patients with alopecia areata, they were able to discover the immune pathways the T cells followed in making their attacks. This led to the discovery of medication called JAK inhibitors that can block the pathways.

Two drugs approved by the FDA were used to regrow the hair completely on mice within twelve weeks. They were ruxolitinib (used to treat a bone marrow disease) and tofacitinib (used to treat rheumatoid arthritis). In a clinical trial conducted at Columbia, patients with hair loss of at least 30 percent were given ruxolitinib. Their hair grew back completely within five months. In addition, those patients no longer had any killer T cells left in their hair follicles. The report on the study was published in 2014.

The genetic links have also helped in diagnosing alopecia areata, as clinics at Columbia now ask patients with diabetes or celiac disease if they have experienced lost hair. About 10 percent of those patients admit they have lost hair in clumps.

The overlap may also aid in the research in the three related diseases. For example, rheumatoid arthritis affects the joints, but it is difficult to biopsy a knee to see what error occurs in the immune response. It is much easier to get a sample of a patient's skin for a biopsy.

Dr. Kevin McElwee, a scientist at the University of British Columbia, has conducted research into one theory about the immune system's role in alopecia areata. Dr. McElwee is examining normal hair follicles and follicles affected by alopecia areata to learn about the basic processes involved in immune privilege. He believes that the genes involved in alopecia areata are not mutations or genes that do not work properly. He thinks

Best Treatment

One way to really help people with alopecia areata is just to treat them with more respect. Do not single them out, as all they really want to do is fit in.

Bob Samuelson was a world-class volleyball player who represented the United States at the 1992 Olympic Games and

Members of the 1992 US Olympic men's volleyball team showed their solidarity with Bob Samuelson by shaving their heads.

at other international events. He started losing his hair in about 1987 and eventually all of it disappeared. He has alopecia universalis.

He said when the hair loss started he refused to go outside. The condition was difficult for him to deal with until his junior or senior year of college. Then he came to accept the condition. He told the *Los Angeles Times* that when someone stares at him now, he will wonder why and then think, "Wait a minute. I'm 6-foot-5 and bald."

During a match in a Latin American country, fans were calling him *bobbia*. When he learned that meant "lightbulb" in Spanish, he smiled and waved to the crowd. He was at the center of a controversy at the Olympics in Barcelona in 1992, but his teammates shaved their heads in a show of unity.

Samuelson told the *Times* that what bothers him most are insensitive comments he hears in the United States.

"There are people who won't say anything to your face, but they will say it loud enough for you to hear it," he said. "People can be very rude. A guy will walk up to me and ask if I have cancer. No, but what if I did? What if I had cancer and only had a couple months to live? How would that make you feel?"

Danielle Garcia donates hair to Locks of Love in 2007. The organization makes high-quality hairpieces for underprivileged people under the age of twenty-one.

that they are probably normally functioning genes that, when they occur together, make a person susceptible to alopecia areata. The **interaction** of genes involved in the condition is being studied. In 2001, Dr. McElwee and Dr. Rolf Huffman discovered that there are cells that can start the growth of mature hair follicles in animals. RepliCel Life Sciences is testing these findings to see if these cells can grow hair on humans.

Another scientist studying the genetics of alopecia areata is Dr. John P. Sundberg, who discovered the mouse model for alopecia areata. He uses mice in his research at the Jackson Laboratory in Bar Harbor, Maine. So far, his studies of mice with alopecia areata have produced detailed information regarding the areas of the mouse genome associated with the disease. He has discovered that drug targets change as alopecia areata develops and progresses. This means that drugs must be used alone or in combinations at different stages of the disease. This development could lead to new treatment options.

Researchers are also developing studies to test the role of **cytokines** in alopecia areata. Interferon gamma is a cytokine that causes the hair follicle to be seen by the immune system and can cause alopecia areata. Researchers think they may be able to use other cytokines to slow or stop the immune system's attack on hair follicles.

A major breakthrough in the treatment of autoimmune diseases was announced in 2014 in the United Kingdom. Scientists there discovered ways to turn off these diseases by stopping the T cells from attacking healthy organs. They selectively targeted cells that cause autoimmune diseases, making them less aggressive and able to protect rather than attack the body.

This is done by injecting fragments of proteins attacked by killer T cells in increasing amounts. This restores tolerance to these proteins, bringing back immune privilege, while leaving the body fully able to fight infection. This antigen-specific immunotherapy is being tested for use on many disorders.

Alopecia areata is an unpredictable disease. Sometimes the hair loss stops and the hair grows back. It can be thin or white at first, but then the hair returns to its original state. If the hair loss is widespread, it is less likely the hair will return.

Some people never lose their hair again, while some people lose and regrow hair for years. This can make the disease very frustrating. Medical advances are providing hope that this cycle of frustration can be ended.

GLOSSARY

amino acid • Acids that occur naturally in living things, some of which form proteins.

anti-inflammatory • Acting to reduce inflammation, which is the pain and swelling that may accompany injury or infection.

atopy • A genetic tendency to develop an allergic reaction such as asthma, hay fever, or eczema.

autoimmune • Having to do with a condition in which the immune system attacks the body itself.

chromosome • The thread-like part of the cell that contains the genes that control hereditary characteristics.

codon • A sequence of three nucleotides that together form a unit of genetic code.

cytokines • Substances such as interferon, interleukin, and growth factors that are secreted by certain cells of the immune system and have an effect on other cells.

disorder • A physical condition that is not normal.

embryo • An unborn or unhatched animal in the earliest stages of development.

genome • The complete set of genes or genetic material present in a cell or organism.

hair follicle • The sheath of cells and connective tissue that surrounds the root of a hair. It gives the hair nourishment.

heredity • The passing on of characteristics from one generation to the next through genes.

hormone • A chemical substance produced inside an animal that controls certain body activities.

hypothesis • A tentative explanation or theory.

immunotherapy • The treatment of a disease by increasing or decreasing the functioning of the immune system.

interaction • How things act upon or influence one another.

liposome • A tiny synthetic sphere used to deliver medicine or drugs.

mange • A skin disease caused by parasitic mites. It causes hair loss, itching, and scabs and can sometimes be passed on to humans.

mutation • A change in a gene. Also, the physical trait that results from such a change.

neuropathic • Relating to neuropathy, which is a degenerative state of the nervous system or of nerves.

parasite • An organism that lives on or in another organism. Parasites get benefits from the host organism but cause harm to it.

polygenic • Involving more than one gene.

spontaneous • Happening without any apparent outside influence.

stem cell • A cell that has the ability to develop into any specialized cell, such as the different types of cells found in a hair follicle.

susceptible • Likely to be affected by something.

symptom • Evidence of a disease.

topical • Applied to the surface of the body.

ultraviolet • Light that the human eye cannot see because the wavelengths are too short. Ultraviolet light from the sun or another source can cause sunburn or even skin cancer.

US Department of Energy • A government agency that addresses the nuclear, energy, and environmental challenges facing the country.

Websites

Bald Girls Do Lunch

www.baldgirlsdolunch.org

This group answers questions, provides links to the latest news, and offers support to women experiencing alopecia areata.

MedicineNet

www.medicinenet.com/alopecia_areata/article.htm

Find the facts about and the treatments for alopecia areata.

WebMD

www.webmd.com/skin-problems-and-treatments/hair-loss/tc/alopecia-areata-topic-overview

Get an overview of alopecia areata and links to stories related to hair loss.

Organizations

American Academy of Dermatology
PO Box 4014
Schaumburg, IL 60168
(866) 503-7546
www.aad.org

National Alopecia Areata Foundation
65 Mitchell Boulevard, Suite 200-B
San Rafael, CA 94903
(415) 472-3780
www.naaf.org

For Further Reading

Boudreau, Gloria. *The Immune System*. San Diego, CA: KidHaven Press, 2004.

Culvert, L. Lee. *Women and Alopecia: Managing Unexpected Hair Loss*. Your Health Press, 2012.

Fitros, Pam. *Boldly Bald Women*. Cookeville, TN: Nightengale Press, 2013.

Fridell, Ron. *Decoding Life: Unraveling the Mysteries of the Genome*. Discovery! Minneapolis, MN: Lerner Publishing Group, 2005.

Hunt, Nigel, and Sue McHale. *Coping with Alopecia*. London: Sheldon Press, 2004.

Murphy-Melas, Elizabeth. *The Girl with No Hair: A Story About Alopecia Areata*. Albuquerque, NM: Health Press, 2003.

Weed, Stacy. *Blond Today, Bald Tomorrow: Living Life With Alopecia Areata*. Owen Sound, ON: The Ginger Press, 2012.

Books

Rubenstein, Irwin. "DNA." *World Book Multimedia Encyclopedia*. Chicago, IL: World Book, 2002.

Rubenstein, Irwin, and Susan M. Wick. "Cell." *World Book Multimedia Encyclopedia*. Chicago, IL: World Book, 2002.

Thompson, Wendy, and Jerry Shapiro. *Alopecia Areata: Understanding and Coping with Hair Loss*. Baltimore, MD: Johns Hopkins University Press, 1996.

Online Articles

Dreifus, Claudia. "Living and Studying Alopecia." *New York Times*. December 27, 2010. Retrieved April 20, 2015. www.nytimes.com/2010/12/28/science/28conversation.html?_r=0

NIH. "Genetic Mapping Fact Sheet." National Human Genome Research Institute. Retrieved April 27, 2015. www.genome.gov/10000715

Price, Vera H. "Therapy of Alopecia Areata: On the Cusp and in the Future." *Journal of Investigative Dermatology Symposium Proceedings*. Retrieved September 2005. www.blackwell-synergy.com/doi/abs/10.1046/ j.1087-0024.2003.00811.x

Sundberg, John P., and Lloyd E. King Jr. "Mouse Alopecia Areata Models: An Array of Data on Mechanisms and Genetics." *Journal of Investigative Dermatology Symposium Proceedings*. Retrieved June 9, 2015. http://www.nature.com/jidsp/journal/v8/n2/full/5640119a.html

Whiteman, Honor. "Baldness Cured With Bone Marrow Disease Drug in Alopecia Areata Patients." *Medical News Today*. August 18, 2014. Retrieved April 27, 2015. www.medicalnewstoday.com/articles/281148.php

Woznicki, Katrina. "Scientists Find Possible Genetic Roots of Type of Hair Loss." *WebMD Health News*. June 30, 2010. Retrieved April 24, 2015. www.webmd.com/skin-problems-and-treatments/hair-loss/news/20100630/scientists-find-possible-genetic-roots-of-alopecia-areata

INDEX

Page numbers in **boldface** are illustrations. Entries in **boldface** are glossary terms.